ETHIOPIA 2016 HUMAN RIGHTS REPORT

EXECUTIVE SUMMARY

Ethiopia is officially a federal republic. The ruling Ethiopian Peoples' Revolutionary Democratic Front (EPRDF), a coalition of four ethnically based parties, controls the government. In May 2015 elections the EPRDF and affiliated parties won all 547 House of People's Representatives seats to remain in power for a fifth consecutive five-year term. In October 2015 parliament elected Hailemariam Desalegn as prime minister. Government restrictions severely limited independent observation of the vote. A mission from the African Union, the sole international institution or organization permitted to observe the voting, called the elections "calm, peaceful and credible." Some nongovernmental organizations (NGOs) reported an environment conducive to free and fair elections was not in place prior to the election. There were reports of unfair government tactics, including intimidation of opposition candidates and supporters, and violence before and after the election that resulted in six confirmed deaths.

Civilian authorities at times did not maintain control over the security forces, and local police in rural areas and local militias sometimes acted independently.

Security forces used excessive force against protesters throughout the year, killing hundreds and injuring many more. The protests were mainly in Oromia and Amhara regions. At year's end more than 10,000 persons were believed still to be detained. This included persons detained under the government-declared state of emergency, effective October 8. Many were never brought before a court, provided access to legal counsel, or formally charged with a crime. On June 10, the government-established Ethiopian Human Rights Commission (EHRC) reported and presented to parliament a summary of its report. The EHRC counted 173 deaths in Oromia, including 28 of security force members and officials, and asserted that security forces used appropriate force there. The EHRC also asserted Amhara regional state special security had used excessive force against the Kemant community in Amhara Region. On August 13, the international NGO Human Rights Watch (HRW) reported an estimate that security forces killed more than 500 protesters. In October the prime minister stated the deaths in Oromia Region alone "could be more than 500." The UN High Commissioner for Human Rights requested access to Oromia and Amhara regions, which the government refused. Following dozens of deaths at a religious festival in Bishoftu on October 2, groups committed property damage. On November 9, international NGO Amnesty International reported more than 800 persons were killed since November 2015.

The most significant human rights problems were security forces' use of excessive force and arbitrary arrest in response to the protests, politically motivated prosecutions, and continued restrictions on activities of civil society and NGOs.

Other human rights problems included arbitrary killings; disappearances; torture and other cruel, inhuman or degrading treatment or punishment; harsh and life-threatening prison conditions; arbitrary arrest, detention without charge, and lengthy pretrial detention; a weak, overburdened judiciary subject to political influence; infringement on citizens' privacy rights, including illegal searches; a lack of participatory consultations and information during the implementation of the government's "villagization" program; restrictions on civil liberties including freedom of speech and press, internet freedom, academic freedom and of cultural events, and freedom of assembly, association, and movement; interference in religious affairs; only limited ability of citizens to choose their government; police, administrative, and judicial corruption; restrictions on activities of civil society and NGOs; violence and societal discrimination against women; female genital mutilation/cutting; abuse of children; trafficking in persons; societal discrimination against persons with disabilities, persons based on their gender identity and sexual orientation, and persons with HIV/AIDS; societal violence including violence based on ethnicity, property destruction, and the killing of security force members; and limits on worker rights, forced labor, and child labor, including forced child labor.

Impunity was a problem. The government generally did not take steps to prosecute or otherwise punish officials who committed abuses other than corruption.

Section 1. Respect for the Integrity of the Person, Including Freedom from:

a. Arbitrary Deprivation of Life and other Unlawful or Politically Motivated Killings

There were numerous reports the government and its agents committed arbitrary and unlawful killings. Security forces used excessive force against protesters throughout the year, killing hundreds. The protests were mainly in Oromia and Amhara regions. A March 14 report from the independent Ethiopian NGO Human Rights Council (HRCO) covering 33 districts in Oromia from November 2015 to February 20 described more than 100 extrajudicial killings. On June 10, the government-established EHRC reported to parliament that it counted 173 deaths in Oromia, including 28 of security force members and officials, and asserted security forces used appropriate force there. The EHRC also asserted Amhara regional state special security had used excessive force against the Kemant community in Amhara Region. The EHRC did not publicly release its report. On August 13, HRW estimated security forces killed more than 500 protesters.

On August 6 and 7, security forces reportedly killed approximately 100 persons in response to demonstrations in major cities and towns across the Oromia and Amhara regions. Political opposition groups reported government forces killed more than 90 protesters in Oromia. The Amhara regional government reported seven deaths; other sources reported more than 50 were killed in Amhara Region.

b. Disappearance

Individuals reportedly arrested by security forces as part of the government's response to protests disappeared. In a June report on the government's response to Oromo protests, HRW reported hundreds of persons were "unaccounted for" including children.

Due to poor prison administration, family members reported individuals missing who were in custody of prison officials, but whom the families could not locate.

c. Torture and Other Cruel, Inhuman, or Degrading Treatment or Punishment

Although the constitution and law prohibit such practices, there were reports security officials tortured and otherwise abused detainees.

In its June report, HRW reported security force members beat detainees, including minors. Security force members used wooden sticks, rubber truncheons, and whips to do so. According to the report, several students stated they were hung by their wrists and whipped, four said they received electric shocks to their feet, and two had weights tied to their testicles. Several female detainees reported security force members raped them. The report stated, "Most of the individuals interviewed by HRW who were detained for more than one month described treatment that appeared to amount to torture."

Mistreatment reportedly occurred at Maekelawi, official detention centers, unofficial detention centers, police stations, and in Kilinto federal prison. There were reports police investigators used physical and psychological abuse to extract confessions in Maekelawi, the federal crime investigation center in Addis Ababa that often held high-profile political prisoners. Interrogators reportedly administered beatings and electric shocks to extract information and confessions from detainees. HRW reported abuses, including torture, that occurred at Maekelawi. In a 2013 report, HRW described beatings, stress positions, the hanging of detainees by their wrists from the ceiling, prolonged handcuffing, pouring of water over detainees, verbal threats, and solitary confinement. Authorities continued to restrict access by diplomats and NGOs to Maekelawi, although some NGOs reported limited access.

The United Nations reported that during the year (as of December 20) it received one allegation of sexual exploitation and abuse against Ethiopian peacekeepers for an incident alleged to have occurred during the year. The allegation, against military personnel deployed to the UN Mission in the Republic of South Sudan, was investigated by the Ethiopian government and found to be unsubstantiated.

Prison and Detention Center Conditions

Prison and pretrial detention center conditions remained harsh and in some cases life threatening. There were reports that authorities beat and tortured prisoners in detention centers, military facilities, and police stations. Medical attention following beatings reportedly was insufficient in some cases. Prisoners died in fires.

The country had six federal and 120 regional prisons. During the state of emergency, effective since October 8, the government announced detention centers in Awash, Ziway, and Dilla and stated suspects could be detained at various police stations in Addis Ababa. There also were many unofficial detention centers throughout the country, including in Dedessa, Bir Sheleko, Tolay, Hormat, Blate, Tatek, Jijiga, Holeta, and Senkele. As part of the government's response to the protests, persons were also detained in military facilities, local administration offices, and makeshift government-owned sites.

A local NGO supported model prisons in Adama, Mekelle, Debre Birhan, Durashe, and Awassa; these prisons had significantly better conditions than those in other prisons.

Pretrial detention often occurred in police station detention facilities, where conditions varied widely, but reports indicated poor hygiene and police abuse of detainees.

<u>Physical Conditions</u>: Authorities sometimes incarcerated juveniles with adults. Prison officials generally separated male and female prisoners, although mixing occurred at some facilities.

Severe overcrowding was common, especially in prison sleeping quarters. The government provided approximately nine birr ($0.40) per prisoner per day for food, water, and health care, although this amount varied across the country. Many prisoners supplemented this amount with daily food deliveries from family members or by purchasing food from local vendors. Other reports noted officials prevented some prisoners from receiving food from their families. Medical care was unreliable in federal prisons and almost nonexistent in regional ones. Prisoners had only limited access to potable water. Water shortages caused unhygienic conditions, and most prisons lacked appropriate sanitary facilities. Many prisoners had serious health problems but received little or no treatment. There were reports prison officials denied some prisoners access to needed medical care. In 2012 the Ministry of Health stated nearly 62 percent of inmates in jails across the country experienced mental health problems due to solitary confinement, overcrowding, and lack of adequate health-care facilities and services.

The June HRW report on government response to Oromo protests stated detainees reported overcrowding, inadequate access to food and water, and solitary confinement, including in military camps. The report stated men and women were not held in the same cells in most locations, but children were detained with adults.

Fires in prisons occurred in Gondar in December 2015, in Ambo on February 19, in Debretabor on September 1, and, on September 3, at Kilinto Prison where at least 23 inmates died.

Visitors of political prisoners and other sources reported political prisoners often faced significantly different treatment compared with other prisoners. Allegations included lack of access to proper medication or any medical treatment, lack of access to books or television, and denial of exercise time. In at least one case, when such complaints were openly raised in a court of law, the presiding judges referred the complaints to the prison administration, which had already refused to look into the complaints.

<u>Administration</u>: Due to the lack of transparency regarding incarceration, it was difficult to determine if recordkeeping was adequate. There were reports prisoners mistreated by prison guards did not have access to prison administrations to

complain. Prisons did not have ombudspersons to respond to complaints. Legal aid clinics existed in some prisons for the benefit of prisoners, and at the regional level had good working relations with judicial, prison, and other government officials. Prison officials allowed detainees to submit complaints to judicial authorities without censorship. Courts sometimes declined to hear such complaints.

The law permits prisoners to have visitors. According to the Anti-Terrorism Proclamation (ATP), a lawyer is permitted to visit only one client per day, and only on Wednesdays and Fridays. Authorities allegedly denied family members access to persons charged with terrorist activity. There were also reports authorities denied the accused visits with lawyers or with representatives of the political parties to which they belonged. In some cases police did not allow pretrial detainees access to visitors, including family members and legal counsel.

After the September 3 fire in the federal prison at Kilinto, attorneys reported visitation for several prisoners was restricted to closely prison visits by family members only. Conversations could not touch on subjects such as trials, politics, and allegations of abuse. This was reported in the prisons in Kilinto, Shewa Robit, and Ziway. These restrictions also applied to political prisoners.

Officials permitted religious observance by prisoners, but this varied by prison, and even by section within a prison, at the discretion of prison management. There were allegations authorities denied detainees adequate locations in which to pray. Prisoners could voice complaints regarding prison conditions or treatment to the presiding judge during their trials.

Independent Monitoring: During the year the International Committee of the Red Cross visited prisons throughout the country as part of its normal activities. The government did not permit access to prisons by other international human rights organizations.

Regional authorities had allowed government and NGO representatives to meet with prisoners without third parties present. By September such allowances were severely curtailed, however. Prison officials reportedly denied access to prisoners for civil society representatives and family members, including in undisclosed locations. The government-established EHRC, which is funded by parliament and subject to parliamentary oversight, monitored federal and regional detention centers and interviewed prison officials and prisoners in response to allegations of widespread human rights abuses. An NGO continued to have access to various prison and detention facilities around the country.

<u>Improvements</u>: The government constructed two new prisons.

d. Arbitrary Arrest or Detention

The constitution and law prohibit arbitrary arrest and detention; however, the state of emergency regulations allowed law enforcement to arrest and detain individuals without a court warrant. There were thousands of reports of arbitrary arrest and detention related to protests. Security forces arbitrarily arrested and detained protesters, professors, university students, musicians, businesspersons, health workers, journalists, children, and others. Security forces went door-to-door after protests to conduct arrests and arbitrarily detained opposition party members and supporters, accusing them of inciting violence.

Role of the Police and Security Apparatus

The Federal Police report to the Office of the Prime Minister and are subject to parliamentary oversight. The oversight was loose. Each of the nine regions has a state or special police force that reports to regional civilian authorities. Local militias operated across the country in loose and varying coordination with regional and federal police and the military. In some cases these militias functioned as extensions of the ruling party. The military played a significant role in responding to the protests. The constitution provides for the military to perform duties assigned to it under a state of emergency.

Impunity remained a serious problem, including impunity for killings of and violence against protesters. The internal mechanisms used to investigate abuses by federal police were not known. On June 10, the government-established Ethiopian Human Rights Commission reported to parliament on the protests, stating it confirmed 173 deaths in Oromia, including 28 security force members and officials, and asserted security forces used appropriate force there. The EHRC also asserted Amhara regional state special security had used excessive force against the Kemant community in Amhara Region. The commission did not publicly release its report. The government rarely publicly disclosed the results of investigations into abuses by local security forces, such as arbitrary detention and beatings of civilians.

The government continued to support human rights training for police and army personnel. It continued to accept assistance from NGOs and the EHRC to improve and professionalize its human rights training and curriculum by including more material on the constitution and international human rights treaties and conventions.

Arrest Procedures and Treatment of Detainees

The constitution and law require detainees be brought to court and charged within 48 hours of arrest or as soon thereafter as local circumstances and communications permit. Travel time to the court is not included in the 48-hour period. With a warrant, authorities may detain persons suspected of serious offenses for 14 days without charge and for additional and renewable 14-day periods if an investigation continues. The courts allowed security officials to continue investigations for more than 14 days without bringing formal charges against suspects.

Under the ATP police may request to detain persons without charge for 28-day periods, up to a maximum of four months, while an investigation is conducted. The law permits warrantless arrests for various offenses including "flagrant offenses." These include offenses in which the suspect was found committing the offense, attempting to commit the offense, or just completing the offense. The ATP permits a warrantless arrest when police reasonably suspect a person has committed or is committing a terrorist act.

The law prohibits detention in any facility other than an official detention center; however, local militias and other formal and informal law enforcement entities used an unknown number of unofficial local detention centers. As part of the government's response to the protests, persons also were detained in military facilities.

A functioning bail system was in place. Bail was not available for persons charged with terrorism, murder, treason, and corruption. In most cases authorities set bail between 500 and 10,000 birr ($22 and $444), which most citizens could not afford. The government provided public defenders for detainees unable to afford private legal counsel but only when cases went to court. There were reports that while some detainees were in pretrial detention, authorities allowed them little or no contact with legal counsel, did not provide full information on their health status, and did not allow family visits. There were reports officials held some prisoners incommunicado for weeks at a time, and civilians were also placed under house arrest for an undisclosed period of time.

The constitution requires authorities under a state of emergency to announce the names of detainees within one month of their arrest. In practice, the names of those detained under the state of emergency were generally announced. The names were not always made available within 30 days and civilians were not always able to locate the rosters of names of those imprisoned.

<u>Arbitrary Arrest</u>: Authorities regularly detained persons arbitrarily, including protesters, journalists, and opposition party members. There were thousands of reports of arbitrary arrest by security forces in response to protests. The March 14 HRCO report listed 84 individuals under "illegal detention," with four having subsequently been released.

On March 8, authorities detained 20 students from Addis Ababa University and charged them under the criminal code with inciting the public through false rumors, holding an illegal demonstration, and encouraging the public to disobey the ATP. On August 1, the Federal First Instance Court acquitted nine of the students and reduced the charges against the 11 others, whose trial continued at year's end.

The government continued to arbitrarily arrest journalists and those who express views that oppose the government (see section 2.a.). On March 3, federal police temporarily detained a foreign correspondent, a freelance journalist, and their translator near Awash Town. Police reportedly took their phones and identification cards and then escorted them back to Addis Ababa. On March 4, authorities released them without giving any explanation for their detention.

In December 2015 police arrested and detained former Blue Party spokesperson Yonatan Tesfaye. On May 4, the federal attorney general charged Yonatan with incitement of terrorism through posts under a pseudonym on Facebook, citing article 4 of the ATP. The court hearing the trial changed the charges to article 6, which pertains to encouragement of terrorism and carries a lesser sentence. Yonatan's trial continued at year's end.

There were developments in the case of three individuals detained in March 2015 at Bole International Airport while on the way to Nairobi. In mid-November a court reduced the charges against Omot Agwa Okwoy to the criminal code and dropped the charges against Ashinie Astin Titoyk, and Jemal Oumar Hojele, who were both released.

<u>Pretrial Detention</u>: Some detainees reported being held for several years without charge or trial. The percentage of the inmate population in pretrial detention and average length of time held was not available. Lengthy legal procedures, large numbers of detainees, judicial inefficiency, and staffing shortages contributed to frequent trial delays. The state of emergency regulations allow authorities to detain a person without a court order until the end of the state of emergency.

<u>Detainee's Ability to Challenge Lawfulness of Detention before a Court</u>: The law provides for detainees to be informed of the nature of their arrest. It also provides persons accused or charged of a crime the ability to appeal. During the year there were no reported cases of a court ruling that a person was unlawfully detained. The law does not provide for persons who are unlawfully detained to receive compensation.

<u>Amnesty</u>: In September, in keeping with a long-standing tradition of issuing pardons at the Ethiopian New Year, the government released more than 12,000 prisoners, including prisoners convicted under the ATP such as Abubeker Ahmed Mohamed and other members of the Muslim Arbitration Committee. Of those, 757 were released from federal prisons and more than 11,000 from regional prisons.

e. Denial of Fair Public Trial

The law provides for an independent judiciary. Although the civil courts operated with a large degree of independence, criminal courts remained weak, overburdened, and subject to political influence. The constitution recognizes both religious and traditional or customary courts.

Trial Procedures

By law accused persons have the right to a fair public trial "without undue delay"; a presumption of innocence; the right to legal counsel of their choice; the right to appeal; the right not to self-incriminate; and the right to present witnesses and evidence in their defense, cross-examine prosecution witnesses, and access government-held evidence. In practice, however, detainees did not always enjoy all these rights, and as a result, defense attorneys were sometimes unprepared to provide an adequate defense. Defendants were not always presumed innocent, able to communicate with an attorney of their choice, provided timely free interpretation as necessary from the moment charged through all appeals, or provided access to government-held evidence. Defendants were often unaware of the specific charges against them until the commencement of their trials. There were reports of detainees being subjected to torture and other abuse while in detention to obtain information or confessions.

The federal Public Defender's Office provided legal counsel to indigent defendants, but scope and quality of service were inadequate due to the shortage of attorneys, who in some cases may individually handle more than 100 cases and many more individual clients at the same time. Numerous free legal aid clinics, based primarily at universities, provided services. In certain areas of the country, the law allows volunteers, such as law students and professors, to represent clients in court on a pro bono basis.

Many citizens residing in rural areas had little access to formal judicial systems and relied on traditional mechanisms for resolving conflict. By law all parties to a dispute must agree to use a traditional or religious court before such a court may hear a case, and either party may appeal to a regular court at any time. Sharia (Islamic law) courts may hear religious and family cases involving Muslims if both parties agree to use a sharia court before going to trial. Sharia courts received some funding from the government and adjudicated a majority of cases in Somali and Afar regions, which are predominantly Muslim. Other traditional systems of justice, such as councils of elders, continued to function. Some women stated they lacked access to free and fair hearings in the traditional court system because local custom excluded them from participation in councils of elders and because of strong gender discrimination in rural areas.

Political Prisoners and Detainees

The number of political prisoners and detainees at years' end was not known. The government detained journalists and political opposition members.

Police arrested Bekele Gerba, deputy chairman of recognized political party the Oromo Federalist Congress (OFC), and 21 others in November and December 2015. On April 22, the attorney general charged them under the ATP. Authorities reportedly mistreated Bekele and others, including denying adequate medical care and access to visitors, including legal counsel. Their trial continued at year's end.

Police arrested other leaders and members of political parties during the year, including Merera Gudina on November 30 (see also section 3, Elections and Political Participation, Political Parties and Political Participation).

There were further updates in the cases of 10 persons including opposition party leaders and others whom police detained in 2014. On May 10, the Federal High Court sentenced Zelalem Workagegnehu to five years and four months in prison, Tesfaye Teferi to three years and 11 months, and Solomon Girma to three years and seven months in prison. The other two defendants in the same trial, Yonatan Wolde and Bahiru Degu, were acquitted and released on April 15. Separately, the prosecution appealed the August 2015 Federal High Court acquittal of Habtamu Ayalew, Yeshiwas Assefa, Daniel Shibeshi, Abraha Desta, and Abraham Solomon. On December 2, the Supreme Court upheld the High Court's acquittal of Habtamu Ayalew, Yeshiwas Assefa, and Abraham Solomon but remanded to the High Court the cases of Daniel Shibeshi and Abraha Desta.

There were also developments in cases of the Zone 9 blogging collective. In October 2015 the Federal High Court acquitted Natnael Feleke, Atnaf Berahane, Abel Wabella, and Soleyana Shimeles Gebremichael (in absentia) and reduced the charges against Befekadu Hailu. The prosecution's appeal of the acquittals continued at the Supreme Court, and the Federal High Court continued to hear the trial of Befekadu Hailu. On October 4, Natnael Feleke was arrested again. He was later released on bail and charged with "inciting the public through false rumors" in relation to having made critical remarks regarding the government during a private conversation at a restaurant. On November 11, authorities arrested Befekadu Hailu again. On December 21, he was released without charge.

Civil Judicial Procedures and Remedies

The law provides citizens the right to appeal human rights violations in civil court. Citizens did not file any such case during the year.

f. Arbitrary or Unlawful Interference with Privacy, Family, Home, or Correspondence

The law generally requires authorities to obtain court-issued search warrants prior to searching private property, however, after the state of emergency, prior court approval for searches was suspended. In an amendment to the state of emergency provisions, security officials had to provide a reason, an official identification card, and be accompanied by someone from the community before conducting a search. The law also recognizes exceptions for "hot pursuit," in which a suspect enters premises or disposes of items that are the subject of an offense committed on the premises, and when police have reasonable suspicion evidence of a crime punishable by more than three years of imprisonment is concealed on or in the property and that a delay in obtaining a search warrant would allow the evidence to be removed. Moreover, the ATP permits warrantless searches of a person or vehicle when authorized by the director general of the Federal Police or his designee or a police officer has reasonable suspicion a terrorist act may be committed and deems a sudden search necessary.

Opposition political party leaders and journalists reported suspicions of telephone tapping, other electronic eavesdropping, and surveillance, and they alleged government agents attempted to lure them into illegal acts by calling and pretending to be representatives of groups--designated by parliament as terrorist organizations--interested in making financial donations.

The government reportedly used a widespread system of paid informants to report on the activities of particular individuals. Opposition members, journalists, and athletes reported ruling party operatives and militia members made intimidating and unwelcome visits to their homes and offices and intimidated family members. These included entry into and searches of homes without a warrant.

There were reports authorities dismissed opposition members from their jobs and that those not affiliated with the EPRDF sometimes had trouble receiving the "support letters" from their kebeles (neighborhoods or wards) necessary to get employment (see section 3, Political Parties and Political Participation).

Security forces continued to detain family members of persons sought for questioning by the government.

The national and regional governments continued to implement the policy of Accelerated Development (informally known as "villagization") plans in the Afar, Benishangul-Gumuz, Gambella, the Southern Nations, Nationalities, and Peoples', Oromia, and Somali regions, which might include resettlement. These plans involved relocation by regional governments of scattered rural populations from arid or semiarid lands vulnerable to recurring droughts into designated communities closer to water, services, and infrastructure. The stated purposes of accelerated development were to improve the provision of government services (health care, education, and clean water), protect vulnerable communities from natural disasters and attacks, and change environmentally destructive patterns of shifting cultivation. Some observers alleged the purpose was to enable large-scale leasing of land for commercial agriculture. The government described the program as strictly voluntary. The government had scheduled to conclude the program in 2015, but decided to continue it.

International donors reported assessments from more than 18 visits to villagization sites since 2011 did not corroborate allegations of systematic, grave human rights violations. They found delays in establishing promised infrastructure and inadequate compensation. Communities and families appeared to have agreed to move based on assurances from authorities of food aid, health and education services, and land; some communities were moved before adequate basic services such as water pumps and shelter were in place in the new locations. Follow-up visits suggested the government had done little to improve consultations with affected communities, and communities were not fully informed when consenting to cede their rights for land projects.

Section 2. Respect for Civil Liberties, Including:

a. Freedom of Speech and Press

The constitution and law provide for freedom of speech and press, however the state of emergency regulations included restrictions on these rights. Authorities harassed, arrested, detained, charged, and prosecuted journalists and others perceived as critical of the government, creating an environment of self-censorship.

Freedom of Speech and Expression: The state of emergency regulations contained several prohibitions that restricted freedom of speech and expression and resulted in detention or disappearance of numerous independent voices. The regulations prohibited any covert or overt agitation and communication that could incite violence and unrest (interpreted to include the popular Oromo protest sign of raising crossed arms over one's head), any communication with designated terrorist groups or antipeace forces, storing and disseminating text, storing and promoting emblems of terrorist groups, incitement in sermons and teaching in religious institutions to induce fear or incite conflict, speech that could incite attacks based on identity or ethnicity, exchange of information by any individual with a foreign government in a manner that undermines national sovereignty and security, and any political parties from briefing journalists in a manner that is anticonstitutional and undermines sovereignty and security. Individuals self-censored as a result of these prohibitions.

Authorities arrested, detained, and harassed persons for criticizing the government. NGOs reported cases of torture of individuals critical of the government. The government attempted to impede criticism through intimidation, including continued detention of journalists and those who express critical opinions online and opposition activists, and monitoring of and interference in activities of political opposition groups. Some feared authorities would retaliate against them for discussing security force abuses. Authorities arrested and detained persons who made statements publicly or privately deemed critical of the government under a provision of the law pertaining to inciting the public through false rumors.

Press and Media Freedoms: The state of emergency prohibited listening to, watching, or reporting information from Ethiopian Satellite Television (ESAT) and Oromo Media Network.

Independent journalists reported problems using government printing presses. Access to private printing presses was scarce to nonexistent.

In Addis Ababa, nine independent newspapers and magazines had a combined weekly circulation of 70,711 copies. Four independent monthly and biweekly magazines published in Amharic and English had a combined circulation of 21,500 copies. State-run newspapers had a combined circulation of 85,500 copies. Most newspapers were printed on a weekly or biweekly basis, except state-owned Amharic and English dailies and the privately run *Daily Monitor*. *Addis Standard* magazine temporarily suspended the print edition of its publication soon after the state of emergency was declared.

Government-controlled media closely reflected the views of the government and ruling EPRDF. The government controlled the only television station that broadcast nationally, which, along with radio, was the primary source of news for much of the population. Six private FM radio stations broadcast in the capital, one private radio station broadcast in the northern Tigray Region, and at least 19 community radio stations broadcast in the regions. State-run Ethiopian Broadcasting Corporation had the largest broadcast range in the country, followed by Fana Radio, which was reportedly affiliated with the ruling party.

The government periodically jammed foreign broadcasts. The law prohibits political and religious organizations and foreigners from owning broadcast stations.

Violence and Harassment: The government continued to arrest, harass, and prosecute journalists. As of mid-December, at least 12 journalists remained in detention.

In December 2015 police detained Fikadu Mirkana, who worked as news anchor and senior reporter for Oromia State TV. He was released in April.

In December 2015 authorities detained journalist Getachew Shiferaw, editor in chief of a web-based opposition-affiliated newspaper. On May 19, authorities charged him with terrorism and his trial continued at year's end.

The trial of two journalists affiliated with Radio Bilal whom authorities arrested in February 2015 and charged with terrorism continued at the Federal High Court.

Censorship or Content Restrictions: Government harassment caused journalists to avoid reporting on sensitive topics. Many private newspapers reported informal editorial control by the government through article placement requests and calls from government officials concerning articles perceived as critical of the government. Private sector and government journalists routinely practiced self-censorship. Several journalists, both local and foreign, reported an increase in self-censorship, especially after the October 8 implementation of the state of emergency. The government reportedly pressured advertisers not to advertise in publications that were critical of the government.

National Security: The government used the ATP to suppress criticism. Journalists feared covering five groups designated by parliament as terrorist organizations in 2011 (Ginbot 7, the Ogaden National Liberation Front (ONLF), the OLF, al-Qaida, and al-Shabaab), citing ambiguity on whether reporting on these groups might be punishable under the law.

Internet Freedom

The government restricted and disrupted access to the internet. It periodically blocked social media sites and internet access in areas of Oromia and Amhara regions, especially during protests. At times the government blocked access throughout the country. There were credible reports the government monitored private online communications without appropriate legal authority. State-owned Ethio Telecom was the only internet service provider in the country.

On June 7, parliament passed the Computer Crime Proclamation. There were concerns its provisions were overly broad and could restrict freedom of speech and expression. This included, for example, a provision that provides for imprisonment for disseminating through a computer system any written, video, audio or any other picture that incites violence, chaos, or conflict among people, and another provision that provides for a prison sentence for intimidation.

In July officials blocked social media sites for days across the country until the national school examination concluded. The government stated blocking these sites was necessary to provide for an "orderly exam process." In May the national exams were reportedly leaked on social media, causing the government to postpone the exams.

On August 6 and 7, the government imposed a nationwide internet blackout.

The state of emergency regulations included prohibited agitation and communication to incite violence and unrest through the internet, text messaging, and social media.

Starting in early October, the government shut down mobile access to the internet in Addis Ababa, most parts of Oromia Region, and other areas. Wired access to several social media and communication sites were also denied. These included social media sites, including Facebook, Twitter, Instagram, YouTube, Skype, WhatsApp, and Viber, news websites such as the *Washington Post* and the *New York Times*, and many other sites, including foreign university homepages and online shopping sites such as Amazon.

The government periodically and increasingly restricted access to certain content on the internet and blocked numerous websites, including blogs, opposition websites, and websites of Ginbot 7, the OLF, and the ONLF, and news sites such as al-Jazeera, the BBC, and RealClearPolitics. Several news blogs and websites run by opposition diaspora groups were not accessible. These included Ethiopian Review, Nazret, CyberEthiopia, Quatero Amharic Magazine, and the Ethiopian Media Forum.

Authorities monitored telephone calls, text messages, and e-mails. Authorities took steps to block access to Virtual Private Network providers that let users circumvent government screening of internet browsing and e-mail. There were reports such surveillance resulted in arrests. According to the International Telecommunication Union, 11.6 percent of the population used the internet in 2015.

In March 2015 Citizen Lab, a Canadian research center at the University of Toronto, reported on attempts in 2014 to infect the computers of U.S.-based employees of ESAT with spyware. ESAT is a diaspora-based television and radio station. According to Citizen Lab, its research suggested involvement of the government and that the attacker may have been the Ethiopian Information and Network Security Agency.

Academic Freedom and Cultural Events

The government restricted academic freedom, including student enrollment, teachers' appointments, and curricula. Authorities frequently restricted speech, expression, and assembly on university and high school campuses. The state of emergency regulations prohibited strikes in educational institutions and closing them or damaging property, gives authorities the power to order educational institutions to take measures against any student or staff member who violates the prohibitions in the regulations, and provides law enforcement the authority to enter educational institutions and take measures to control strikes or protests.

The ruling party, via the Ministry of Education, continued to favor students loyal to the party in assignment to postgraduate programs. Some university staff members commented that students who joined the party received priority for employment in all fields after graduation.

Authorities limited teachers' ability to deviate from official lesson plans. Numerous anecdotal reports suggested non-EPRDF members were more likely to be transferred to undesirable posts and bypassed for promotions. There were reports of teachers not affiliated with the EPRDF being summarily dismissed for failure to attend party meetings. There continued to be a lack of transparency in academic staffing decisions, with numerous complaints from academics alleging bias based on party membership, ethnicity, or religion.

A separate Ministry of Education directive prohibits private universities from offering degree programs in law and teacher education. The directive also requires public universities to align their curriculum with the ministry's policy of a 70/30 ratio between science and social science academic programs. As a result the number of students studying social sciences and the humanities at public institutions continued to decrease; private universities focused heavily on the social sciences.

Reports indicated a pattern of surveillance and arbitrary arrests of Oromo university students based on suspicion of their holding dissenting opinions or participation in peaceful demonstrations. According to reports there was an intense buildup of security forces (uniformed and plainclothes) embedded on university campuses preceding student protests, especially in Oromia, and in response to student demonstrations.

b. Freedom of Peaceful Assembly and Association

Freedom of Assembly

The constitution and law provide for freedom of assembly; the state of emergency regulations, however, prohibited demonstrations and town hall meetings that did not have approval from the command post, the entity that oversees the state of emergency. The government did not respect freedom of assembly and killed, injured, detained, and arrested numerous protesters throughout the year (see also sections 1.a., 1.b., 1.c., 1.d., and 1.e.). The majority of protests were in Oromia and Amhara regions. On August 13, HRW reported an estimate that security forces killed more than 500 protesters since November 2015. On January 21 and October 10, UN experts called on the government to end the "crackdown on peaceful protests." The UN High Commissioner for Human Rights requested access to the regions, which the government did not provide. On November 9, Amnesty international estimated at least 800 had been killed.

On August 6 and 7, security forces reportedly killed approximately 100 persons in response to simultaneous demonstrations in major cities and towns across Oromia and Amhara regions (see section 1.a).

On October 2, dozens were reportedly killed at a religious festival in Bishoftu. Security forces' response to agitation in the crowd, including the use of teargas and firing into the air, reportedly led to a stampede that left many dead. On October 7, the UN Office of the High Commissioner for Human Rights (OHCHR) called for an investigation and urged the government allow independent observers access to Oromia and Amhara regions. On October 10, a group of UN human rights experts highlighted the October 2 events and urged the government to allow an international commission of inquiry to investigate the protests and violence used against protesters since November 2015. The government-established EHRC conducted an investigation into the incident. The results of that investigation were unknown.

Prior to the state of emergency, organizers of public meetings of more than two persons or demonstrations had to notify the government 48 hours in advance and obtain a permit. Authorities could not refuse to grant a permit but could require the event be held at a different time or place for reasons of public safety or freedom of movement. If authorities determined an event should be held at another time or place, the law required organizers be notified in writing within 12 hours of the time of submission of their request. After the state of emergency, prior-issued permits were deemed invalid.

Prior to the state of emergency, the government denied some requests by opposition political parties to hold protests but approved others. Opposition party organizers alleged government interference in most cases, and authorities required several of the protests be moved to different dates or locations from those the organizers requested. Protest organizers alleged the government's claims of needing to move the protests based on public safety concerns were not credible. Local government officials, almost all of whom were affiliated with the EPRDF, controlled access to municipal halls, and there were many complaints from opposition parties that local officials denied or otherwise obstructed the scheduling of opposition parties' use of halls for lawful political rallies. There were numerous credible reports owners of hotels and other large facilities cited internal rules forbidding political parties from utilizing their spaces for gatherings. Regional governments, including the Addis Ababa regional administration, were reluctant to grant permits or provide security for large meetings. After the state of emergency, the prohibition on unauthorized demonstrations or town hall meetings limited the organization of meetings, training sessions, and other gatherings. For example, members of at least one opposition political party reported they were prevented from having a four-person meeting.

Freedom of Association

Although the law provides for freedom of association and the right to engage in unrestricted peaceful political activity, the government severely limited this right (see sections 3 and 5).

The state of emergency and the accompanying regulations restricted the ability of organizations to operate (see also section 5). The prohibitions relating to communication and acts that undermine tolerance and unity resulted in self-censorship of reports and public statements. The prohibition on unauthorized town hall meetings limited the organization of meetings, training sessions, and other gatherings. The prohibition on exchanging information or contact with a foreign government or NGOs in a manner that undermines national sovereignty and security reduced communication between local organizations and international organizations and others.

The state of emergency regulations also prohibited any political party "from briefing local or foreign journalists in a manner that is anticonstitutional and undermining sovereignty and security."

The Charities and Societies Proclamation (CSO) law bans anonymous donations to NGOs. All potential donors were therefore aware their names would be public knowledge. The same was true concerning all donations made to political parties.

A 2012 report by the UN special rapporteur on the rights to freedom of peaceful assembly and association stated, "The enforcement of these (the CSO law) provisions has a devastating impact on individuals' ability to form and operate associations effectively."

International NGOs seeking to operate in the country had to submit an application via the country's embassies abroad, which the Ministry of Foreign Affairs then submitted to the Charities and Societies Agency for approval.

c. Freedom of Religion

See the Department of State's *International Religious Freedom Report* at www.state.gov/religiousfreedomreport/.

d. Freedom of Movement, Internally Displaced Persons, Protection of Refugees, and Stateless Persons

Although the law provides for freedom of internal movement, foreign travel, emigration, and repatriation, the state of emergency regulations restricted internal movement. The government also restricted freedom of internal movement and foreign travel.

The government cooperated with the Office of the UN High Commissioner for Refugees (UNHCR) and other humanitarian organizations in providing protection and assistance to internally displaced persons (IDPs), refugees, returning refugees, asylum seekers, stateless persons, and other persons of concern. At times authorities or armed groups limited the ability of humanitarian organizations to operate in areas of insecurity, such as on the country's borders.

In-country Movement: The state of emergency regulations prohibited diplomats from travelling more than 25 miles outside of Addis Ababa without prior notification to and approval from the command post. The government lifted this restriction in early November. Security concerns forced a temporary halt of deliveries of food and other humanitarian assistance in limited areas in Amhara and Oromia regions.

<u>Foreign Travel</u>: A 2013 ban on unskilled workers travelling to the Middle East for employment continued. The ban did not affect citizens travelling for investment or other business reasons. The government stated it issued the ban to prevent harassment, intimidation, and trauma suffered by those working abroad, particularly in the Middle East, as domestic employees.

There were several reports of authorities restricting foreign travel, similar to the following case: On March 23, National Intelligence and Security Service officials at Bole International Airport in Addis Ababa prevented Merera Gudina, chairman of the OFC, from departing the country. On June 15, Merera was permitted to leave. Authorities arrested him on December 1.

Authorities restricted travel of persons in the Zone 9 case. For example, authorities confiscated blogger Zelalem Kibret's passport in November 2015 and prevented him from boarding his international flight. Airport security officials said he could not leave the country because he had previously been arrested. Authorities returned Zelalem's passport on June 1, and he was later permitted to travel abroad.

<u>Exile</u>: As in past years, citizens including journalists and others remained abroad in self-imposed exile due to fear of government retribution should they return.

Internally Displaced Persons

According to the International Organization for Migration (IOM), there were 684,064 IDPs between August 2015 and August, including protracted and new cases, many of them due to the impact of the El Nino weather phenomenon. This was an increase compared with previous years.

Of the IDPs, 397,296 were displaced by flooding and conflict while 188,244 were displaced due to the effects of the drought related to El Nino. Another 33,300 were displaced due to resource-based competition. Most of those affected by El Nino returned to their places of origin.

IOM estimated 657, 224 individuals were considered "protracted IDPs," meaning they lacked durable solutions such as local integration, internal resettlement, or return to home. The reasons for protracted displacements included interclan and cross-border conflict, natural disasters, political or community considerations in IDP resettlements, and lack of resettlement resources. Of these IDPs, 283,092 resided in Somali Region; 148,482 in Afar; 144,295 in Oromia; 47,950 in the Southern Nations, Nationalities, and Peoples' Region; 13,245 in Amhara; 2,290 in Dire Dawa; and 2,055 in Harar. An additional 15,815 individuals displaced by flooding were still on the move and thus could not be attributed to any one region.

IOM reported in August 41,316 individuals or 7,844 households were internally displaced in Amhara, Oromia, and Somali regions, due to conflict and flooding. From August 24 through mid-September, approximately 8,000 individuals moved from Amhara Region to northwestern Tigray Region. Many of the IDPs cited as the reason for their departure recent conflicts in the region and a generalized sense they could be targeted because of their ethnicity (Tigrayan). The federal government allocated six million birr ($266,361) to Tigray Region for the IDP response. The funds were distributed among Hemera, Axum, Mekele, and Shire, which were the towns with the greatest IDP influx. The largest volume of arrivals was in Shire, which received 2.6 million birr ($115,423) of the region's total. The federal government established a committee led by the Tigray Regional Agriculture Department to seek permanent integration options for the IDPs.

The IOM estimated an April 15 attack in Gambella Region by Murle ethnic group from South Sudan displaced more than 21,000 individuals (see section 6, Other Societal Violence or Discrimination).

The government, through the Disaster Risk Management Food Security Sector (DRMFSS), continued to play an active role in delivering humanitarian assistance to IDPs. Federal and local DRMFSS officials coordinated with IOM and its partners in monitoring IDP populations.

Protection of Refugees

Access to Asylum: The law provides for granting of asylum or refugee status, and the government has established a system for providing protection to refugees. The state of emergency regulations prohibited entering the country without a visa.

According to UNHCR, the country hosted 743,732 refugees as of August. The majority of refugees were from South Sudan (281,612) and Somalia (254,277), with others from Eritrea (161,615), Sudan (39,317), and other countries. There were 1,554 registered Yemeni asylum seekers.

UNHCR, the Administration for Refugee and Returnee Affairs, and humanitarian agencies continued to care for Sudanese arrivals fleeing from conflict in Sudan's Blue Nile State, averaging 1,500 new arrivals per month, according to UNHCR. The government also extended support to asylum seekers from South Sudan, mostly arriving from Upper Nile and Unity states. Persistent conflict and food insecurity prompted the flow of South Sudanese refugees into the country; there were an estimated 2,712 arrivals during August.

Eritrean asylum seekers continued to arrive. Approximately 23 percent were unaccompanied minors. Many who arrived regularly departed for secondary migration through Egypt and Sudan to go to Europe and other final destinations.

Freedom of movement: The state of emergency regulations prohibited leaving refugee camps without permission from an authorized body. The government continued a policy that allowed some Eritrean refugees to live outside a camp. The government gave such permission primarily for persons to attend higher-education institutions, undergo medical treatment, or avoid security threats at the camps.

Employment: The government does not grant refugees work permits.

Durable Solutions: The government welcomed refugees to settle in the country but did not offer a path to citizenship or provide integration. The government supported a policy allowing some refugees to live outside camps and engage in informal livelihoods. Refugee students who passed the required tests could attend university with fees paid by the government and UNHCR.

Section 3. Freedom to Participate in the Political Process

The constitution and law provide citizens the ability to choose their government in free and fair periodic elections held by secret ballot and based on universal and equal suffrage. The ruling party's electoral advantages, however, limited this ability.

Elections and Political Participation

Recent Elections: In May 2015 the country held national elections for the House of People's Representatives, the country's parliamentary body. In October 2015 parliament re-elected Hailemariam Desalegn prime minister.

In the May 2015 national parliamentary elections, the EPRDF and affiliated parties won all 547 seats, giving the party a fifth consecutive five-year term. Government restrictions severely limited independent observation of the vote. The African Union was the sole international organization permitted to observe the elections. Opposition party observers accused local police of interference, harassment, and extrajudicial detention. Independent journalists reported little trouble covering the election, including reports from polling stations. Some independent journalists reported receiving their observation credentials the day before the election, after having submitted proper and timely applications. Six rounds of broadcast debates preceded the elections, and for the most part they were broadcast in full and only slightly edited. The debates included all major political parties. Several laws, regulations, and procedures implemented since the 2005 national elections created a clear advantage for the EPRDF throughout the electoral process. In addition the "first past the post" provision, or 50 percent plus one vote required to win a seat in parliament, as stipulated in the constitution, contributed to EPRDF's advantage in the electoral process. There were reports of unfair government tactics, including intimidation of opposition candidates and supporters. Various reports confirmed at least six election-related deaths during the period before and immediately following the elections. The National Electoral Board of Ethiopia (NEBE) is politically dependent on the prime minister, and there is no opportunity for nonruling political parties to have a say in its decisions concerning party registration and candidate qualification. NEBE has sole responsibility for voter education and broadcast radio segments and distributed manuals on voter education in many local languages.

In a preliminary election assessment, the African Union called the elections "calm, peaceful, and credible" and applauded the government for its registration efforts. It raised concerns, however, regarding the legal framework underpinning the election. NEBE registered more than 35 million voters, and did not report any incidents of unfair voter registration practices.

<u>Political Parties and Political Participation</u>: The government, controlled by the EPRDF, unduly restricted political parties and members of certain ethnic groups, particularly the Amhara and Oromo, who stated they lacked genuine political representation at the federal level. The state of emergency regulations restricted political parties' ability to operate. For example, the regulations prohibit any political party "from briefing local or foreign journalists in a manner that is anticonstitutional and undermining sovereignty and security."

Authorities arrested and prosecuted political opposition members including under allegations of terrorism (see section 1.e., Political Prisoners). Government officials alleged many members of legitimate Oromo opposition parties were secretly OLF members and, more broadly, that members of many opposition parties had ties to Ginbot 7.

The OFC reported that authorities have kept OFC general secretary Bekele Nega under house arrest since December 30, 2015. Security personnel reportedly told him not to leave his house in Addis Ababa, use his phone, or give any interviews to media. Authorities also arrested other OFC leaders and members including Merera Gudina and Bekele Gerba (see section 1.e., Denial of Fair Public Trial, Political Prisoners and Detainees).

On October 11, authorities arrested Blen Mesfin and three other members of the registered Blue (Semayawi) Party. Blen Mesfin was charged with "inciting the public through false rumors." Authorities ordered her release on bail. On the day scheduled for her release, authorities rearrested and detained her without charge. She was released on December 21, although it was unclear whether she still faced charges.

Constituent parties of the EPRDF conferred advantages upon their members; the parties directly owned many businesses and were broadly perceived to award jobs and business contracts to loyal supporters. Several opposition parties reported difficulty in renting homes or buildings in which to open offices, citing visits by EPRDF members to the property owners to persuade or threaten them not to rent property to these parties. There were reports authorities terminated the employment of teachers and other government workers who belonged to opposition political parties. According to Oromo opposition groups, the Oromia regional government continued to threaten to dismiss opposition party members, particularly teachers, from their jobs. There were reports unemployed youths not affiliated with the ruling coalition sometimes had trouble receiving the "support letters" from their wards necessary to get jobs.

Registered political parties must receive permission from regional governments to open and occupy local offices. Opposition parties reported difficulty acquiring the required permissions for regional offices, adversely affecting their ability to organize and campaign. Laws requiring parties to report "public meetings" and obtain permission for public rallies were also used to inhibit opposition activities.

Participation of Women and Minorities: No laws prevented women or minorities from voting or participating in political life, although highly patriarchal customs in some regions limited female participation in political life. Women were significantly underrepresented in both elected and appointed positions. As of the October change in cabinet assignments, women held three of the 22 federal government ministerial positions, including one of three deputy prime minister positions, and also held 212 of 547 seats in the national parliament. The Tigray Regional Council included the highest proportion of women nationwide, at 50 percent (76 of the 152 seats).

The government's policy of ethnic federalism led to the creation of individual constituencies intended to provide for representation of all major ethnic groups in the House of Federation (one of the two chambers of parliament). There were more than 80 ethnic groups, and small groups lacked representation in the other chamber of parliament, the House of People's Representatives.

Section 4. Corruption and Lack of Transparency in Government

The law provides criminal penalties for corruption by officials. Despite the government's prosecution of some officials for corruption, many officials continued to engage in corrupt practices with impunity. Although the government cited fighting corruption as a high priority in its public statements, there were perceptions corruption increased in the government.

Corruption: Corruption, especially the solicitation of bribes, including police and judicial corruption, remained problems. Some government officials were thought to manipulate the land allocation process, and state- and party-owned businesses received preferential access to land leases and credit. The federal attorney general was mandated to investigate and prosecute corruption cases.

The government attributed some of the unrest in Oromia to corruption. For example, on June 9, authorities detained Zelalem Jemaneh, former head of the Oromia Regional State Agriculture Bureau with the rank of deputy chief administrator, on allegations of corruption.

The trial of Wondimu Biratu Kena'a, former head of the Revenues Bureau of Oromia Region who was arrested in August 2015 on allegations of grand corruption and embezzlement, continued at year's end.

On May 17, the High Court sentenced former intelligence deputy chief Woldeselassie Woldemichael, who authorities arrested in 2013, to 10 years in prison and a fine of 50,000 birr ($2,220) after convicting him of abuse of power and generation of wealth from unknown sources.

Financial Disclosure: The law requires all government officials and employees to register their wealth and personal property. The law includes financial and criminal sanctions for noncompliance. The president and prime minister registered their assets. The Federal Ethics and Anti-Corruption Commission (FEACC) reported it registered the assets of 26,584 appointees, officials, and employees between July 2015 and April. The commission also carried out reregistration of previously registered assets in the stated period. As of November 2015, 95,000 officials had registered their assets as required by law.

The FEACC held financial disclosure records. By law any person who seeks access to these records may make a request in writing; access to information on family assets may be restricted unless the FEACC deems the disclosure necessary.

Public Access to Information: The law provides for public access to government information, but access was largely restricted. The law includes a narrow list of exceptions outlining the grounds for nondisclosure. Responses generally must be made within 30 days of a written request, and fees may not exceed the actual cost of responding to the request. The law includes mechanisms for punishing officials for noncompliance, as well as appeal mechanisms for review of disclosure denials. Information on the number of disclosures or denials during the year was not available.

The government publishes laws and regulations in its national gazette, known as the *Federal Negarit Gazeta*, prior to their taking effect. The Government Communications Affairs Office managed contacts between the government, the press, and the public; the private press reported the government rarely responded to its queries.

Section 5. Governmental Attitude Regarding International and Nongovernmental Investigation of Alleged Violations of Human Rights

A few domestic human rights groups operated but with significant government restrictions. The government was generally distrustful and wary of domestic and international human rights groups and observers. State-controlled media were critical of international human rights groups such as HRW.

The CSO law prohibits charities, societies, and associations (NGOs or CSOs) that receive more than 10 percent of their funding from foreign sources from engaging in activities that advance human and democratic rights or promote equality of nations, nationalities, peoples, genders, and religions; the rights of children and persons with disabilities; conflict resolution or reconciliation; or the efficiency of justice and law enforcement services. The law severely curtails civil society's ability to raise questions of good governance, human rights, corruption, and transparency and forced many local and international NGOs working on those issues to either cease advocacy, or reregister and focus on activities other than rights-based advocacy.

Some human rights defender organizations continued to register either as local charities, meaning they could not raise more than 10 percent of their funds from foreign donors but could act in the specified areas, or as resident charities, which allowed foreign donations above 10 percent but prohibited advocacy activities in those areas.

The state of emergency and the accompanying regulations restricted the ability of organizations to operate. The prohibitions relating to communication and acts that undermine tolerance and unity resulted in self-censorship of reports and public statements. The prohibition on unauthorized town hall meetings limited the organization of meetings, training sessions, and other gatherings. The prohibition on exchanging information or contact with a foreign government or NGOs in a manner that undermines national sovereignty and security reduced communication between local organizations and international organizations and others. Curfews in certain areas impeded human rights investigations. The obligation of all organizations to give information when asked by law enforcement raised concerns regarding confidentiality of information.

In July, August, and October, authorities arrested seven members of HRCO. On October 23, authorities dispersed a fundraising event celebrating HRCO's 25th anniversary. Authorities claimed the organization did not seek additional approval from the command post for the gathering, though it had sought and received approval for the event prior to the start of the state of emergency. As of November 27, at least three members of HRCO remained in detention.

The government denied most NGOs access to federal prisons, police stations, and undisclosed places of detention. The government permitted a local NGO that has an exemption enabling it to raise unlimited funds from foreign sources and to engage in human rights advocacy to visit prisoners. Some NGOs played a positive role in improving prisoners' chances for clemency.

Authorities limited access of human rights organizations, media, humanitarian agencies, and diplomatic missions in certain areas.

The government continued to lack a clear policy on NGO access to sensitive areas, leading regional government officials and military officials frequently to refer requests for NGO access to the federal government. Officials required journalists to register before entering certain regions or denied access. There were reports of regional police or local militias blocking NGO access to particular locations on particular days, citing security concerns.

The United Nations or Other International Bodies: The government did not cooperate with requests for investigations from the OHCHR or UN experts. In August the UN High Commissioner for Human Rights urged the government to allow independent observers into Oromia and Amhara regions. The commissioner reportedly said allegations of excessive use of force across the two regions must be investigated. The government dismissed the request through its spokesperson, who, on August 11, told an international media the United Nations was entitled to its opinion, but the government was responsible for the safety of its own citizens. The spokesperson stated the government would launch its own investigation. On October 7, following the deaths at the religious festival in Bishoftu, the OHCHR reiterated the request the government allow independent observers access to Oromia and Amhara regions. On October 10, a group of UN human rights experts urged the government to allow an international commission of inquiry to investigate.

Requests from the UN special rapporteur on torture and other cruel, inhuman, or degrading treatment or punishment to visit the country remained unanswered.

Government Human Rights Bodies: The EHRC reportedly investigated hundreds of human rights complaints, organized field investigations, conducted prison visits to provide recommendations on improving prison conditions, and produced annual and thematic reports. On June 10, the EHRC reported to parliament that it counted 173 deaths in Oromia, including 28 of security force members and officials, and asserted security forces used appropriate there. The EHRC also asserted Amhara regional state special security had used excessive force against the Kemant community in Amhara Region. The commission did not publicly release its report. The EHRC also investigated the September 3 fire in Kilinto prison. The commission operated 112 legal aid centers in collaboration with 22 universities and two civil society organizations, the Ethiopian Women Lawyers' Association, and the Ethiopian Christian Lawyers Fellowship.

The Office of the Ombudsman has authority to investigate complaints of administrative mismanagement by executive branch offices. From July 2015 to June, the office received 2,849 complaints; the ombudsman opened investigations into 1,231 (including 209 cases from the previous year) and referred 1,827 cases outside its mandate to other offices. Of the 1,231 cases the office investigated, it reported resolving 1,010 (82 percent); 221 remained pending. The majority of complaints investigated dealt with land, administration of public service, delay in service delivery, unjust decisions, social security, and access to information.

Section 6. Discrimination, Societal Abuses, and Trafficking in Persons

Women

Rape and Domestic Violence: The law criminalizes rape and provides for penalties of five to 20 years' imprisonment, depending on the severity of the case. The law does not expressly address spousal rape. The government did not fully enforce the law, partially due to widespread underreporting. Recent statistics on the number of abusers prosecuted, convicted, or punished were not available.

Domestic violence is illegal, but government enforcement of laws was inconsistent. Domestic violence, including spousal abuse, was a pervasive social problem. Depending on the severity of damage inflicted, penalties range from small fines to up to 15 years' imprisonment.

Although women had recourse to police and the courts, societal norms and limited infrastructure prevented many women from seeking legal redress, particularly in rural areas. The government prosecuted offenders on a limited scale.

Domestic violence and rape cases often were delayed significantly and given low priority. In the context of gender-based violence, significant gender gaps in the justice system remained, due to poor documentation and inadequate investigation. Gender-based violence against women and girls was underreported due to cultural acceptance, shame, fear of reprisal, or a victim's ignorance of legal protections.

"Child friendly" benches hear cases involving violence against children and women. Police officers were required to receive domestic violence training from domestic NGOs and the Ministry of Women, Children, and Youth Affairs. There was a commissioner for women and children's affairs on the EHRC.

Female Genital Mutilation/Cutting (FGM/C): FGM/C is illegal, but the government did not actively enforce this prohibition or punish those who practiced it. According to the UN Children's Fund (UNICEF), 74 percent of women and girls had undergone FGM/C. The penal code criminalizes the practice of clitoridectomy, with sentences of imprisonment of at least three months or a fine of at least 500 birr ($22). Infibulation of the genitals is punishable by five to 10 years' imprisonment. No criminal charges, however, have ever been filed for FGM/C.

The prevalence of FGM/C was reportedly declining. UNICEF cited a 2011 Welfare Monitoring Survey as finding 23 percent of girls between birth and age 14 had undergone FGM/C. Although statistics on FGM/C varied, one report from 2013 cited Afar, Somali, and Dire Dawa regions as having the highest prevalence of FGM/C. It was less common in urban areas.

The age at which FGM/C is performed depends on the ethnic group, type of FGM/C performed, and region. In the north FGM/C tended to be performed immediately after birth; in the south, where FGM/C is more closely associated with marriage, it was performed later. Girls typically had clitoridectomies performed on them seven days after birth (consisting of an excision of the clitoris, often with partial labial excision) and infibulation (the most extreme and dangerous form of FGM/C) at the onset of puberty. The government's strategy was to discourage the practice through education in public schools, the Health Extension Program, and broader mass media campaigns rather than to prosecute offenders. International bilateral donors and private organizations were active in community education efforts to reduce the prevalence of FGM/C, following the government's lead of sensitization rather than legal enforcement.

Other Harmful Traditional Practices: Marriage by abduction is illegal, although it continued in some regions despite the government's attempts to combat the practice. Forced sexual relationships accompanied most marriages by abduction, and women often experienced physical abuse during the abduction. Abductions led to conflicts among families, communities, and ethnic groups. In cases of abduction, the perpetrator did not face punishment if the victim agreed to marry the perpetrator.

<u>Sexual Harassment</u>: Sexual harassment was widespread. The penal code prescribes penalties of 18 to 24 months' imprisonment, but authorities generally did not enforce harassment laws.

<u>Reproductive Rights</u>: Individuals and couples generally have the right to decide the number, spacing, and timing of their children; manage their reproductive health; and to have access to the information and means to do so, free from discrimination, coercion, or violence. Traditional practices such as marriage by abduction in which forced sex occurred limited this right in practice. According to a 2016 Demographic and Health Survey (DHS), the maternal mortality rate declined to 412 deaths per 100,000 live births. An article surveying maternal mortality listed obstructed labor/uterine rupture, hemorrhage, hypertensive disorders of pregnancy, and sepsis/infection as the top four causes from 2000 to 2012. The 2016 DHS found a modern contraceptive prevalence rate of 35 percent nationwide among married women and 55 percent among sexually active unmarried women. For married women the rate increased compared with that found in previous DHS surveys. According to the 2016 DHS, the percentage of births delivered by a skilled attendant increased to 28 percent and those that occurred in a health facility increased to 26 percent. Abortion is illegal but with numerous exceptions. The incidence of illegal, unsafe abortions had declined since legislation changed, which accounted in part for the drop in maternal mortality. All maternal and child health services were provided free of charge in the public sector; however, challenges persisted in accessing quality services in more remote areas of the country due to transportation problems.

<u>Discrimination</u>: Discrimination against women was a problem and was most acute in rural areas, where an estimated 80 percent of the population lived. The law contains discriminatory regulations, such as the recognition of the husband as the legal head of the family and the sole guardian of children more than five years old. Courts generally did not consider domestic violence by itself a justification for granting a divorce. Irrespective of the number of years a marriage existed, the number of children raised, and joint property, the law entitled women to only three months' financial support if a relationship ended. There was limited legal recognition of common-law marriage. A common-law husband had no obligation to provide financial assistance to his family, and consequently women and children sometimes faced abandonment. Traditional courts continued to apply customary law in economic and social relationships.

The constitution states ownership of land and natural resources "is exclusively vested in the State and in the peoples of Ethiopia." Both men and women have land-use rights that they may pass on as an inheritance. Land law varies among regions, however. All federal and regional land laws empower women to access government land. Inheritance laws also enable widows to inherit joint property they acquired during marriage.

In urban areas women had fewer employment opportunities than men did, and the jobs available did not generally provide equal pay for equal work. Women's access to gainful employment, credit, and the opportunity to own or manage a business was limited by their generally lower level of education and training and by traditional attitudes.

Children

Birth Registration: Citizenship is derived from one's parents. The law requires all children to be registered at birth. Children born in hospitals were registered; most of those born outside of hospitals were not. The overwhelming majority of children, particularly in rural areas, were born at home. During the year the government initiated a campaign to increase birth registrations.

Education: The law does not make education compulsory. As a policy primary education was universal and tuition free; however, there were not enough schools to accommodate the country's youth, particularly in rural areas. The cost of school supplies was prohibitive for many families. The number of students enrolled in schools expanded faster than trained teachers could be deployed. The net primary school enrollment rate was 90 percent of boys and 84 percent of girls

Child Abuse: Child abuse was widespread. Uvula cutting, tonsil scraping, and milk tooth extraction were amongst the most prevalent harmful traditional practices. *The African Report on Child Wellbeing 2013*, published by the African Child Policy Forum, found the government had increased punishment for sexual violence against children. "Child friendly" benches heard cases involving violence against children and women. There was a commissioner for women and children's affairs in the EHRC.

Early and Forced Marriage: The law sets the legal marriage age for girls and boys at 18; however, authorities did not enforce this law uniformly, and rural families sometimes were unaware of this provision. In several regions it was customary for older men to marry girls, although this traditional practice continued to face greater scrutiny and criticism. The government strategy to address underage marriage focused on education and mediation rather than punishment of offenders.

According to a 2015 UNICEF report, 16 percent of women ages 20-24 were married before age 15 and 41 percent before age 18. According to the 2011 DHS, the median age of first marriage among women between ages 20 and 49 who were surveyed was 17.1 years, compared with 16.5 years in 2005.

In Amhara and Tigray regions, girls were married as early as age seven. Child marriage was most prevalent in Amhara Region, where approximately 45 percent of girls marry before age 18, and the median first marriage age was 15.1 years, according to the 2011 DHS, compared with 14.7 years in 2005. Regional governments in Amhara and, to a lesser extent, Tigray offered programs to educate girls, young women, parents, community leaders, and health professionals on problems associated with early marriage.

Female Genital Mutilation/Cutting (FGM/C): Information is provided in the women's section above.

Sexual Exploitation of Children: The minimum legal age for consensual sex is 18, but authorities did not enforce this law. The law provides for three to 15 years in prison for sexual intercourse with a minor. The law provides for one year in prison and a fine of 10,000 birr ($444) for trafficking in indecent material displaying sexual intercourse by minors. The law prohibits profiting from the prostitution of minors and inducing minors to engage in prostitution; however, commercial sexual exploitation of children continued, particularly in urban areas. Girls as young as age 11 were reportedly recruited to work in brothels. Customers often sought these girls because they believed them to be free of sexually transmitted diseases. Young girls were trafficked from rural to urban areas. They also were exploited as prostitutes in hotels, bars, resort towns, and rural truck stops. Reports indicated family members forced some young girls into prostitution.

Infanticide or Infanticide of Children with Disabilities: Ritual and superstition-based infanticide, including of infants with disabilities, continued in remote tribal areas, particularly South Omo. Local governments worked to educate communities against the practice.

Displaced Children: According to a 2010 report by the Ministry of Labor and Social Affairs, approximately 150,000 children lived on the streets, of whom 60,000 were in the capital. The ministry's report stated the inability of families to support children due to parental illness or insufficient household income exacerbated the problem. Research in 2014 by the ministry noted rapid urbanization, illegal employment brokers, high expectations of better life in cities, and rural-urban migration were adding to the problem. These children begged, sometimes as part of a gang, or worked in the informal sector. A large number of unaccompanied minors from Eritrea continued to arrive in the country (see section 2.d.).

Institutionalized Children: There were an estimated 4.5 million orphans in the country in 2012, according to statistics published by UNICEF. The vast majority lived with extended family members. Government and privately run orphanages were overcrowded, and conditions were often unsanitary. Due to severe resource constraints, hospitals and orphanages often overlooked or neglected abandoned infants. Institutionalized children did not receive adequate health care.

International Child Abductions: The country is not a party to the 1980 Hague Convention on the Civil Aspects of International Child Abduction. See the Department of State's *Annual Report on International Parental Child Abduction* at travel.state.gov/content/childabduction/en/legal/compliance.html.

On April 15, members of the Murle ethnic group from South Sudan reportedly abducted more than 100 children from Gambella Region (see section 6, Other Societal Violence or Discrimination).

Anti-Semitism

The Jewish community numbered approximately 2,000 persons. There were no reports of anti-Semitic acts.

Trafficking in Persons

See the Department of State's *Trafficking in Persons Report* at www.state.gov/j/tip/rls/tiprpt/.

Persons with Disabilities

The constitution does not mandate equal rights for persons with disabilities. The law prohibits discrimination against persons with physical and mental disabilities in employment and mandates access to buildings but does not explicitly mention intellectual or sensory disabilities. It is illegal for deaf persons to drive.

The law prohibits employment discrimination based on disability. It also makes employers responsible for providing appropriate working or training conditions and materials to persons with disabilities. The law specifically recognizes the additional burden on women with disabilities. The government took limited measures to enforce the law, for example, by assigning interpreters for deaf and hard of hearing civil service employees (see section 7.d.). The Ministry of Labor and Social Affairs and the Public Servants Administration Commission are responsible for the implementation of the Proclamation on The Rights of Disabled Persons to Employment.

The law mandates building accessibility and accessible toilet facilities for persons with physical disabilities, although specific regulations that define the accessibility standards were not adopted. Buildings and toilet facilities were usually not accessible. Property owners are required to give persons with disabilities preference for ground-floor apartments, and this was respected.

Women with disabilities were more disadvantaged than men with disabilities in education and employment. The 2010 Population Council Young Adult Survey found young persons with disabilities were less likely to have ever attended school than those without disabilities. The survey indicated girls with disabilities were less likely than boys to be in school: 23 percent of girls with disabilities were in school, compared with 48 percent of girls and 55 percent of boys without disabilities. Overall, 48 percent of young persons with disabilities surveyed reported not going to school due to their disability. Girls with disabilities also were much more likely to suffer physical and sexual abuse than girls without disabilities. Of sexually experienced girls with disabilities, 33 percent reported having experienced forced sex. According to the same survey, approximately 6 percent of boys with disabilities had been beaten in the three months prior to the survey, compared with 2 percent of boys without disabilities.

There were several schools for persons with hearing and vision disabilities and several training centers for children and young persons with intellectual disabilities. There was a network of prosthetic and orthopedic centers in five of the nine regional states.

The Ministry of Labor and Social Affairs worked on disability-related problems. The CSO law continued to affect negatively several domestic associations, such as the Ethiopian National Association of the Blind, the Ethiopian National Association of the Deaf, and the Ethiopian National Association of the Physically Handicapped, as it did other civil society organizations. International organizations and some local CSOs were active, particularly on issues concerning accessibility and vocational training for persons with disabilities.

The right of persons with disabilities to vote and otherwise participate in civic affairs is not restricted by law, although lack of accessibility can make participation difficult. In the May 2015 national elections, African Union observers reported voters requiring assistance were always provided with assistance, either by a person of their choice or by polling staff. Most polling stations were accessible to persons with disabilities, and priority was given to them as well as to the elderly, pregnant women, and nursing mothers.

National/Racial/Ethnic Minorities

The country has more than 80 ethnic groups, of which the Oromo, at approximately 35 percent of the population, is the largest. The federal system drew boundaries approximately along major ethnic group lines. Most political parties remained primarily ethnically based, although the ruling party and one of the largest opposition parties are coalitions of ethnically based parties.

HRCO reported that a few Oromo protesters in Ameya, South West Shoa Zone of Oromia, burnt down homes and property of Amhara residents on December 12, 2015. According to the HRCO report, the attack displaced several hundred farmers and destroyed more than 800 homes. A number of Amhara farmers reportedly retaliated by burning down homes of 96 Oromo farmers. The two communities held joint meetings and condemned the attacks on both sides. They were working together to rebuild the destroyed houses.

Acts of Violence, Discrimination, and Other Abuses Based on Sexual Orientation and Gender Identity

Consensual same-sex sexual activity is illegal and punishable by three to 15 years' imprisonment. No law prohibits discrimination against lesbian, gay, bisexual, transgender, and intersex (LGBTI) individuals. There were some reports of violence against LGBTI individuals; reporting was limited due to fear of retribution, discrimination, or stigmatization. There are no hate crime laws or other criminal justice mechanisms to aid in the investigation of abuses against LGBTI individuals. Individuals did not identify themselves as LGBTI persons due to severe societal stigma and the illegality of consensual same-sex sexual activity. Activists in the LGBTI community stated they were followed and at times feared for their safety. There were no updates on reports of persons incarcerated for allegedly engaging in same-sex sexual activities.

The AIDS Resource Center in Addis Ababa reported the majority of self-identified gay and lesbian callers, most of whom were men, requested assistance in changing their behavior to avoid discrimination. Many gay men reported anxiety, confusion, identity crises, depression, self-ostracism, religious conflict, and suicide attempts.

HIV and AIDS Social Stigma

Societal stigma and discrimination against persons with or affected by HIV/AIDS continued in the areas of education, employment, and community integration. Persons with or affected by HIV/AIDS reported difficulty accessing various services. There were no statistics on the scale of the problem.

Other Societal Violence or Discrimination

Violence occurred, including in Gambella Region and during protests.

On April 15, armed men from the Murle ethnic group from South Sudan who crossed into the country reportedly killed more than 200 women and children in three woredas of Nuer Zone in Gambella Region. The attackers also reportedly abducted more than 100 children and stole thousands of cattle. The Murle attack added to the instability of the region, which was already under pressure because of interethnic clashes between Nuer and Anuak groups that started on January 20.

On April 21, South Sudanese refugees living in Jewi camp in Gambella Region reportedly killed 10 Ethiopians contracted by an international NGO to build a secondary education facility. The violence was triggered when an NGO-contracted truck hit and killed two refugee children. Authorities detained 53 refugees suspected of the killings and, on August 15, filed criminal charges against 23 of them. According to the Administration for Refugee and Returnee Affairs, the government provided two public defenders to represent the refugees at their trial. The UNHCR Protection Unit as well as the International Committee of the Red Cross had access to the detainees and monitored the legal process.

On June 29, residents of Hana Mariam, Furi, and Mango Cheffe localities of Nifas Silk Laphto Subcity in Addis Ababa clashed with police and killed two police officers and a local official during the start of the city government's operation to evict residents forcibly. Both Addis Ababa Police Commission and Government Communication Affairs Office confirmed the killings.

Section 7. Worker Rights

a. Freedom of Association and the Right to Collective Bargaining

The constitution and law provide workers, except for civil servants and certain categories of workers primarily in the public sector, with the right to form and join unions, conduct legal strikes, and bargain collectively, although other provisions and laws severely restrict or excessively regulate these rights. The law specifically prohibits managerial employees, teachers, health-care workers, judges, prosecutors, security-service workers, domestic workers, and seasonal and part-time agricultural workers from organizing unions.

A minimum of 10 workers is required to form a union. While the law provides all unions with the right to register, the government may refuse to register trade unions that do not meet its registration requirements including because of a nonpolitical conviction of the union leader within the previous 10 years and the presence of illegal union objectives. The government may unilaterally cancel the registration of a union. Workers may not join more than one trade union per employment. The law stipulates a trade union organization may not act in an overtly political manner. The law allows administrative authorities to appeal to the courts to cancel union registration for engaging in prohibited activities, such as political action.

Other laws and regulations that explicitly or potentially infringe upon workers' rights to associate freely and to organize include the CSO law, Council of Ministers Regulation No. 168/2009 on Charities and Societies to reinforce the CSO law, and the ATP. The International Labor Organization (ILO) Committee of Experts on the Application of Conventions and Recommendations noted the CSO law gives the government power to interfere in the right of workers to organize, including through the registration, internal administration, and dissolution of organizations' processes.

While the law recognizes the right of collective bargaining, this right was severely restricted. Negotiations aimed at amending or replacing a collective agreement must be completed within three months of its expiration; otherwise, the provisions on wages and other benefits cease to apply. Civil servants, including public school teachers, have the right to establish and join professional associations created by the employees but not to negotiate better wages or working conditions. Arbitration procedures in the public sector are more restrictive than those in the private sector. The law does not provide for effective and adequate sanctions against acts of interference by other agents in the establishment, functioning, or administration of either workers' or employers' organizations.

Although the constitution and law provide workers with the right to strike to protect their interests, the law contains detailed provisions prescribing extremely complex and time-consuming formalities that make legal strike actions difficult. The law requires aggrieved workers to attempt reconciliation with employers before striking and includes a lengthy dispute settlement process. These provisions apply equally to an employer's right to lock workers out. Two-thirds of the workers concerned must support a strike before it is authorized. If a case has not already been referred to a court or labor relations board, workers retain the right to strike without resorting to either of these options, provided they give at least 10 days' notice to the other party and the Ministry of Labor and Social Affairs and make efforts at reconciliation.

The law also prohibits strikes by workers who provide essential services, including air transport and urban bus service workers, electric power suppliers, gas station personnel, hospital and pharmacy personnel, firefighters, telecommunications personnel, and urban sanitary workers. The list of essential services exceeds the ILO definition of essential services. The law prohibits retribution against strikers, but it also provides for civil or penal penalties against unions and workers involved in unauthorized strike actions. Violation of this procedure is an offense punishable with a fine not exceeding 1,200 birr ($53) if committed by a union or of 300 birr ($13) if committed by an individual worker. If the provisions of the penal code prescribe more severe penalties, the punishment laid down in the code becomes applicable. The government may dissolve unions for carrying out strikes in "essential services."

The informal labor sector, including domestic workers, was not unionized and was not protected by labor laws. Workers are defined as persons in an employment relationship. Lack of adequate staffing prevented the government from effectively enforcing applicable laws for those sectors protected by law. Court procedures were subject to lengthy delays and appeals.

Freedom of association and the right to collective bargaining were respected, but some legal problems remained. The ILO was critical of the government's alleged use of the antiterrorism law to punish ringleaders, organizers, or commanders of forbidden societies, meetings, and assemblies. The government refused for the fourth year to register the National Teachers Union (NTA) on grounds a national teachers' association already existed and that the NTA's registration application was not submitted in accordance with the CSO law. In 2013 an ILO mission made a working visit and signed a joint statement with the Ministry of Labor and Social Affairs, stating the government was committed to registering the NTA. The ILO's Ethiopia office reiterated this message and characterized the dispute as an administrative issue focused on naming rights and diaspora membership.

While the government allowed citizens to exercise the right of collective bargaining, enterprise unions are allowed to negotiate wages only at the plant level. Unions in the formal industrial sector made some efforts to enforce labor regulations.

Antiunion activities occurred but were rarely reported. Despite the law prohibiting antiunion discrimination, unions reported employers terminated union activists. There were unconfirmed reports that some major foreign investors generally did not allow workers to form unions, often transferred or dismissed union leaders, and intimidated and pressured members to leave unions. Lawsuits alleging unlawful dismissal often took years to resolve because of case backlogs in the courts. Employers found guilty of antiunion discrimination were required to reinstate workers dismissed for union activities and generally did so. The law prohibits retribution against strikers, and there were no reported cases of violations. Labor officials reported that high unemployment, fear of retribution, and long delays in hearing labor cases deterred workers from participating in strikes or other labor actions.

b. Prohibition of Forced or Compulsory Labor

In August 2015 the federal government enacted a comprehensive overhaul of its antitrafficking penal code. The code prescribes harsh penalties of up to life imprisonment and a fine of 500,000 birr ($22,197) for human trafficking and exploitation, including slavery, debt bondage, forced prostitution, and servitude.

Although the ban on labor migration to the Gulf States remained in effect, in February the government enacted the Revised Overseas Employment Proclamation (Proclamation No. 923/20 16), a major precondition for lifting the labor migration ban.

The law prohibits all forms of forced or compulsory labor but permits courts to order forced labor as a punitive measure. Slavery, even in disguised form, is punishable with five to 20 years' imprisonment and a fine. The government did not effectively enforce the law, and forced labor occurred. Police at the federal and regional levels began to receive training focused on human trafficking and exploitation. Both adults and children were forced to engage in street vending, begging, traditional weaving, or agricultural work. Children also worked in forced domestic labor. Situations of debt bondage also occurred in traditional weaving, pottery making, cattle herding, and other agricultural activities, mostly in rural areas. Girls were exploited in domestic servitude and prostitution in neighboring African countries. Ethiopian women who migrated for work or fled abusive employers in the Middle East were also vulnerable to sex trafficking. Men and boys migrated to the Gulf States and other African nations, where some were subjected to forced labor.

The government sometimes deployed prisoners to work outside the prisons for private businesses, a practice the ILO stated could constitute compulsory labor.

Also see the Department of State's *Trafficking in Persons Report* at www.state.gov/j/tip/rls/tiprpt/.

c. Prohibition of Child Labor and Minimum Age for Employment

By law the minimum age for wage or salary employment is 14. The minimum age provisions, however, apply only to contractual labor and do not apply to self-employed children or children who perform unpaid work. The law prohibits hazardous or night work for children between 14 and 18. The law defines hazardous work as any work that could jeopardize a child's health. Prohibited work sectors include passenger transport, work in electric generation plants, factory work, underground work, street cleaning, and many other sectors. The law expressly excludes children under age 16 attending vocational schools from the prohibition on hazardous work. The law does not permit children between ages 14 and 18 to work more than seven hours per day, between 10 p.m. and 6 a.m., or on public holidays or rest days.

Child labor remained a serious problem. The small number of trained labor inspectors and a lack of enforcement resources resulted in numerous violations. Occupational safety and health measures were not effectively enforced, and significant numbers of children worked in prohibited work sectors, particularly construction.

School enrollment was low, particularly in rural areas. To underscore the importance of attending school, joint NGO and government-led community-based awareness-raising efforts targeted communities where children were heavily engaged in agricultural work. The government invested in modernizing agricultural practices and constructing schools to combat the problem of child labor in agricultural sectors.

In both rural and urban areas, children often began working at young ages. Child labor was particularly pervasive in subsistence agricultural production, traditional weaving, fishing, and domestic work. A growing number of children worked in construction. Children in rural areas, especially boys, engaged in activities such as cattle herding, petty trading, plowing, harvesting, and weeding, while other children, mostly girls, collected firewood and fetched water. Children worked in the production of gold. In small-scale gold mining, they dug mining pits and carried heavy loads of water. Children in urban areas, including orphans, worked in domestic service, often working long hours, which prevented many from attending school regularly. Children also worked in manufacturing, shining shoes, making clothes, parking, public transport, petty trading, as porters, and directing customers to taxis. Some children worked long hours in dangerous environments for little or no wages and without occupational safety protection. Child laborers often faced physical, sexual, and emotional abuse at the hands of their employers.

Also see the Department of Labor's *Findings on the Worst Forms of Child Labor* at www.dol.gov/ilab/reports/child-labor/findings/.

d. Discrimination with Respect to Employment and Occupation

The law prohibits discrimination based on race, ethnicity, national origin nationality, gender, marital status, religion, political affiliation, political outlook, pregnancy, socioeconomic status, disability, or "any other conditions." The law specifically recognizes the additional burden on pregnant women and persons with disabilities (see section 6). Sexual orientation, gender identity, and HIV-positive status are not specifically protected. The penalty for discrimination on the above grounds is a fine of 1,200 birr ($53). The government took limited measures to enforce the law.

Discrimination in employment and occupation occurred with respect to women, who had fewer employment opportunities than did men, and the jobs available did not provide equal pay for equal work.

Discrimination against migrant workers also occurred (see section 7.e.).

e. Acceptable Conditions of Work

There is no national minimum wage. Some government institutions and public enterprises set their own minimum wages. Public-sector employees, the largest group of wage earners, earned a monthly minimum wage of approximately 420 birr ($19). The official estimate for the poverty income level was 315 birr ($14) per month.

Only a small percentage of the population, concentrated in urban areas, was involved in wage-labor employment. Wages in the informal sector generally were below subsistence levels.

The law provides for a 48-hour maximum legal workweek with a 24-hour rest period, premium pay for overtime, and prohibition of excessive compulsory overtime. The country has 13 paid public holidays per year. The law entitles employees in public enterprises and government financial institutions to overtime pay; civil servants receive compensatory time off for overtime work. The government, industries, and unions negotiated occupational safety and health standards. Workers specifically excluded by law from unionizing, including domestic workers and seasonal and part-time agricultural workers, generally did not benefit from health and safety regulations in the workplace.

The Ministry of Labor and Social Affairs' inspection department was responsible for enforcement of workplace standards. In 2015 the country had 423 labor inspectors and, according to the ministry, they completed 37,500 inspections in 2015. The labor inspectors did not enforce standards effectively. The ministry's severely limited administrative capacity; lack of an effective mechanism for receiving, investigating, and tracking allegations of violations; and lack of detailed, sector-specific health and safety guidelines hampered effective enforcement of these standards. Maximum penalties for different types of violations range from 300 birr ($13) to 1,000 birr ($44), which by themselves are insufficient to deter such violations

Compensation, benefits, and working conditions of seasonal agricultural workers were far below those of unionized permanent agricultural employees. The government did little to enforce the law. Most employees in the formal sector worked a 39-hour workweek. Many foreign, migrant, and informal-sector workers worked more than 48 hours per week.

Workers have the right to remove themselves from dangerous situations without jeopardizing their employment; there were no reports that workers exercised this right. Hazardous working conditions existed in the agricultural sector, which was the primary base of the country's economy. There were also reports of hazardous and exploitative working conditions in the construction and industrial sectors, although data on deaths and injuries were not available.